Caterpillars

CLAIRE LLEWELLYN • BARRIE WATTS

W
FRANKLIN WATTS
A Division of Scholastic Inc.
NEW YORK TORONTO LONDON AUCKLAND SYDNEY
MEXICO CITY NEW DELHI HONG KONG
DANBURY, CONNECTICUT

First published in 2000 by Franklin Watts
96 Leonard Street, London EC2A 4XD

First American edition 2002 by Franklin Watts
A Division of Scholastic Inc.
90 Sherman Turnpike
Danbury, CT 06816

Text and artwork © 2000 Franklin Watts
Photography © 2000 Barrie Watts

Series Editor: Anderley Moore
Editor: Rosalind Beckman
Series Designer: Jason Anscomb
Designer: Joelle Wheelwright
Illustrator: David Burroughs

Catalog details are available from the Library of Congress
Cataloging-in-Publication Data

ISBN 0-531-14656-1 (lib. bdg.) 0-531-14830-0 (pbk.)

Printed in Hong Kong/China

Contents

What Are Caterpillars?

Caterpillars are the wriggly little grubs that hatch out of the eggs of a butterfly or a moth. Caterpillars look nothing like their parents. This is because butterflies and moths go through four different stages as they grow. Being a caterpillar is the second stage of their life cycle.

This is the caterpillar of the Indian moon moth.

The life cycle of a swallowtail butterfly

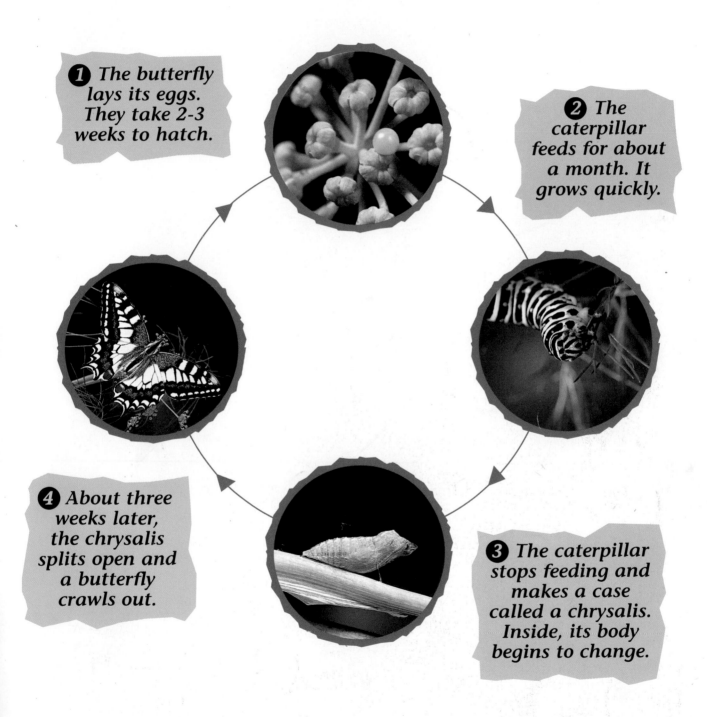

1 The butterfly lays its eggs. They take 2-3 weeks to hatch.

2 The caterpillar feeds for about a month. It grows quickly.

4 About three weeks later, the chrysalis splits open and a butterfly crawls out.

3 The caterpillar stops feeding and makes a case called a chrysalis. Inside, its body begins to change.

Hatching

Moths and butterflies lay their eggs on the leaves of plants. The eggs are tiny and well hidden. The parents always choose plants that their young can eat as soon as they hatch out of the egg.

These eggs are laid out of sight, hidden under a cabbage leaf. The leaf will give the caterpillars food when they hatch.

When it is ready to hatch, the caterpillar bites its way out of the egg. It waves its head back and forth as it pulls the rest of its tiny body free. Then it is ready for a meal. First it eats its eggshell. Then it starts on the leaf!

Caterpillars are tiny and pale when they first hatch.

A Caterpillar's Body

There are about 150,000 different kinds of caterpillar. They can be dull or brightly colored with spots and stripes. Their body can be smooth or covered in bristles or hair. All caterpillars are the same sort of shape, and have the same parts to their body.

◄ *The green coloring of the caterpillar of the privet hawk moth helps it blend in with its surroundings.*

▲ *The caterpillar of the tropical moth is very hairy.*

The brightly-colored caterpillar of the spurge hawkmoth ▼

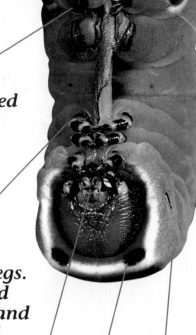

A caterpillar's body is long and soft, and made up of segments. At one end of the body is the head. On the head is the spinneret. This is a small hole that produces silk. At the other end of the body are pairs of claspers, which the caterpillar uses to cling to leaves.

The extra sucker-like legs are called claspers or prolegs.

The front three pairs of legs are called true legs. They are used for walking and holding food.

The jaws are big and strong.

The simple eyes can only tell light from dark.

The head is inside a hard shell.

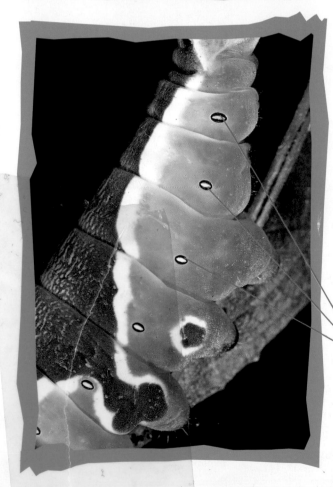

Caterpillars breathe through their spiracles. These are tiny holes on the side of the body that let in oxygen.

Moving Along

A caterpillar moves up and down like waves. Over and over again, the caterpillar lets go of the leaf with each set of legs, then stretches forward and clasps hold again.

A caterpillar's claspers are very strong. Each one has a band of tiny hooks, which can easily grip rough surfaces.

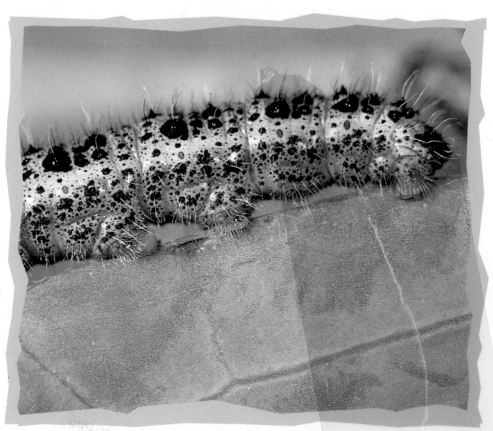

❶ Looper caterpillars such as the caterpillar of the magpie moth move in a different way. First, they make a loop with their body to bring their back legs up to the front.

❷ Then they let go with the front legs and stretch forward.

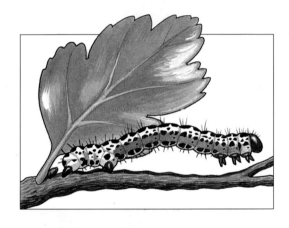

❸ They make another loop as they bring up the rear.

Caterpillars cannot fly like their parents, but a few do move through the air. They drop down on a line of silk, like a spider, and wait for a gust of wind to lift them and carry them along.

Feeding

Caterpillars are eating machines. Day and night, in spring and summer, they munch on the leaves of plants. Caterpillars can quickly strip a plant, leaving nothing but a skeleton of stalks.

Caterpillars have large jaws for their body size because leaves are hard to eat.

Many caterpillars are fussy eaters and feed on only one kind of plant. This means that different sorts of caterpillars can live side by side in the same place without running out of food.

▲ *Caterpillars of the tortoiseshell butterfly feed only on nettles.*

◄ *Some caterpillars are named after their favorite foods! Caterpillars of the cabbage white butterfly feed only on cabbage leaves.*

Growing Bigger

Caterpillars have a very thin skin. As they grow bigger, their skin gets tight and begins to split. This is called molting.

When a caterpillar has molted, the old, empty skin is left hanging on a leaf.

❶ *When a caterpillar is ready to molt, it stops feeding and hides itself away somewhere safe.*

❷ *It spins a small silk pad and holds on tightly. Soon its skin begins to split.*

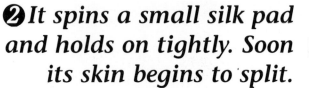

❸ *The caterpillar crawls forward, leaving its old skin behind.*

❹ *The caterpillar starts to feed again. Its new, larger skin will allow it to grow.*

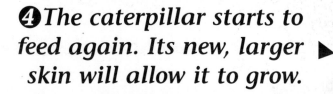

Enemies

Caterpillars are plump, juicy, and very slow. They make easy pickings for sharp-eyed birds. Every spring, thousands of caterpillars end up as meals for chicks. They are a very important food.

Not just birds feed on caterpillars. So do mice, shrews, frogs, snakes, beetles, and other insects.

Even ants enjoy a caterpillar meal.

Some wasps feed caterpillars to their young. Others lay their eggs inside caterpillars. When the wasps hatch, they feed on the caterpillar.

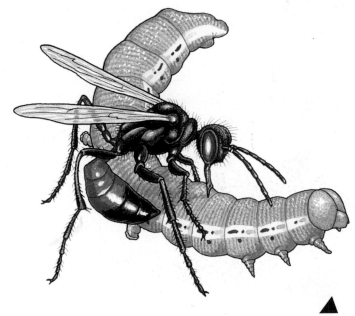

A wasp lays its eggs inside a caterpillar of a clouded sulphur butterfly.

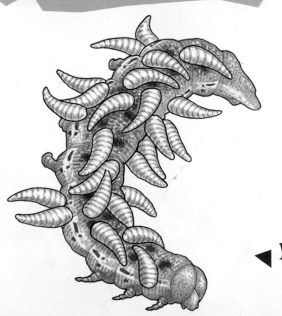

Young wasp larvae feeding on their caterpillar home

Don't Eat Me!

Caterpillars have many ways of defending themselves. Some have a skin color that helps hide them. Others look bad, smell bad, or have a nasty taste. A few have bristles that prickle or sting, or long hairs that leave a rash.

The caterpillar of the orchard swallowtail butterfly has the perfect disguise. It looks just like a bird dropping.

The markings and eye spots of a puss moth caterpillar help to scare its enemies. ▶

The caterpillar of the elephant hawkmoth ◀ is a spotted green color. On plants it is very hard to see.

The woolly bear caterpillar makes a hairy mouthful. Most creatures leave it alone. ▶

Changing Shape

When a caterpillar is fully grown, it is ready to become a butterfly. It molts its skin one last time and then turns into a chrysalis. The chrysalis is a case that protects the caterpillar as its body changes shape.

❶ The large white caterpillar gets ready to molt.

❷ As its skin splits, the creature wriggles free. Underneath is the soft chrysalis.

❸ The outside of the chrysalis soon hardens. Inside, the caterpillar's body begins to change.

Chrysalises are usually hard to find. They can look like dead leaves (A) or bark (B). They can be hidden under leaves (C) or even under windowsills (D).

A. Common sailor butterfly chrysalis

4 *A butterfly crawls out of its chrysalis.*

5 *The butterfly will rest for a while before flying away.*

Some butterflies crawl out of the chrysalis after two to three weeks, but others stay inside until spring.

B. Queen page swallowtail butterfly chrysalis

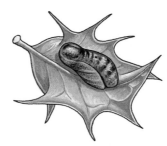

C. Holly blue butterfly chrysalis

D. Small tortoiseshell butterfly chrysalises

Spinning a Cocoon

The caterpillars of moths do not make chrysalises. They spin a silky cocoon instead. Some caterpillars weave scraps of leaf or bark in with the silk. This helps the cocoon blend in with the background and makes it harder to see.

❶ The caterpillar of the American moon moth attaches itself to a leaf and begins to wrap itself in silk.

❷ When the cocoon is finished, it is well hidden by the leaf.

This cocoon has been ▶ *cut away to show the caterpillar inside.*

Caterpillar Crazy!

In the first 56 days of its life, the caterpillar of the polyphemus moth eats 86,000 times its own weight in leaves. That is like a human baby eating six large truckloads of food.

Some caterpillars (such as those of the monarch butterfly or Cinnabar moth) feed on poisonous plants. The poison does not kill them, but makes them poisonous to their enemies. It is a very clever defense.

A looper caterpillar has a clever disguise. It looks just like a twig.

Some caterpillars spin a silk tent to hide themselves as they feed.

The silkworm is the caterpillar of the bombyx mori moth. About 4,000 years ago, the Chinese learned to unravel its cocoons and weave the thread into silk.

The silkworm caterpillar makes its cocoon from just one very long silk thread. It measures about one-half mile from end to end.

The caterpillars of pine processionary moths like to stick together. They crawl around the forest in single file, in a procession (line) up to five and one-half yards long.

Caterpillars can be a real pest. Some of them feed on fruit trees. Others enjoy corn, potato, and tomato plants.

In parts of Australia and Africa, caterpillars are roasted and eaten as snacks.

Every spring, some kinds of bird collect about 16,000 caterpillars to feed their young.

Although caterpillars are able to spin thread, butterflies cannot. They do not have a spinneret.

Glossary

chrysalis   the hard case that forms around a caterpillar before it changes into a butterfly (plural: chrysalises)

claspers   the pairs of sucker-like legs that caterpillars use for walking and clinging to leaves and branches

cocoon   the silky case that a caterpillar spins when it is ready to change into a moth

life cycle   all the different stages that an animal goes through in life

molt   to shed a skin in order to grow larger

spinneret   the hole on a caterpillar that lets out silk

spiracles   the small holes along a caterpillar's body that it uses to breathe

true legs   the front three pairs of legs a caterpillar uses for walking and holding food

Index